Explore!
Chocolate

Liz Gogerly

Published in paperback in 2014 by Wayland
Copyright © Wayland 2015

Wayland
338 Euston Road
London NW1 3BH

Wayland Australia
Level 17/207 Kent Street
Sydney, NSW 2000

Editors: Vicky Brooker and Julia Adams
Designer: Elaine Wilkinson
Picture Researcher: Shelley Noronha
Illustrations for step-by-steps: Peter Bull

British Library Cataloguing in Publication Data
Chocolate. -- (Explore!)
1. Chocolate--Juvenile literature.
I. Series
641.3'374-dc23

ISBN 978 0 7502 8379 3

Printed in Malaysia

10 9 8 7 6 5 4 3 2

Wayland is a division of Hachette Children's
Books, an Hachette UK company
www.hachette.co.uk

Picture acknowledgements:
The author and publisher would like to thank the
following agencies and people for allowing these
pictures to be reproduced:

p. 1 (LH image) & p. 27: AFP/Getty Images;
p. 1 (RH image) & p. 23: AFP/Getty Images;
p. 4: PoodlesRock/Corbis; p. 5 (both images)
& p. 31): choccywoccydoodah; p. 8: Olivier
Polet/Corbis; p. 11: ullsteinbild/TopFoto; p.
12: Ann Johansson/Corbis; p. 13 (top): Jessica
Dimmock/VII Network/Corbis; p. 13 (bottom):
Imagebroker/Alamy; p. 14: George H.H. Huey/
Corbis; p. 15 (top): Mexican School/Getty
Images; p. 15 (bottom): akg-images/album/
Oronoz; p. 16: akg-images/album/Oronoz; p. 17
(top): Historical Picture Archive/Corbis; p. 18:
Mary Evans Picture Library/Alamy; p. 19 (top):
The Granger Collection/TopFoto; p. 19 (bottom):
The Art Archive / Bodleian Library Oxford (shelf
mark JJ Choc & Confectionery 1); p. 23 (bottom):
Jose MAnuel Ribeiro/X00727/Reuters/Corbis; p.
26 (LH image): India Today Group/Getty Images;
p. 26 (RH image): AFP/Getty Images; p. 29 (top
RH image): Vicki Beaver/Alamy; p. 29 (bottom RH
image): St Andrews Preservation Trust Museum;
All other images and creative graphics:
Shutterstock

Contents

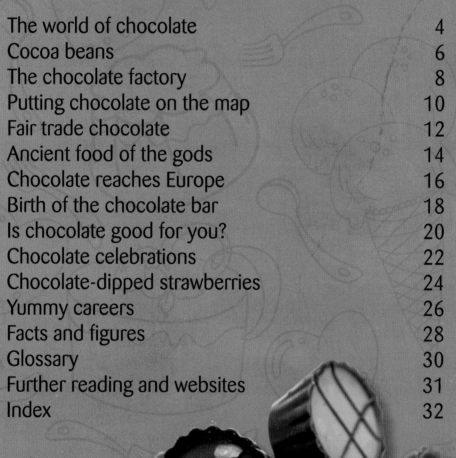

The world of chocolate

Chocolate is a treat enjoyed by millions of people around the world. It is the main ingredient in lots of snacks and sweets. It is also added to cakes, cookies, biscuits, ice cream and puddings.

Chocolate houses

People were drinking chocolate long before they were tucking into chocolate bars and sweets. The ancient Mayans drank it over 2,000 years ago, and after Spain invaded Central America in the sixteenth century, chocolate became fashionable in parts of Europe, too. By the seventeenth century, chocolate houses were a little like modern-day coffee shops, but still only chocolate drinks were on the menu. At this time, chocolate was an exotic foodstuff enjoyed by people in high society.

A Victorian advertisement for drinking chocolate.

Bars, boxes and beyond

It wasn't until Victorian times that milk and sugar were added to chocolate to create the kind of chocolate bars we know today. Now, chocolate comes in more varieties than ever before, and all kinds of ingredients are added. In addition to chocolate bars and drinks, products range from seasonal treats, such as Easter eggs, to boxes of handmade chocolates and even chocolate fountains.

Chocolate really does come in all shapes and sizes - even huge colourful cakes and skulls!

Cocoa beans

The chocolate we eat is made from cocoa beans. These beans are found inside cocoa pods that grow on cocoa trees. The scientific name for the cocoa tree is *Theobroma cacao*, and it is native to South America.

The cocoa tree

Although cocoa trees originally come from South America, they are now cultivated around the world in hot tropical places. These small evergreen trees look a little like English apple trees. They grow best under a canopy of larger trees where they are shaded from the Sun and wind. The tree grows to just over eight metres. A mature tree is covered in tiny pink and white flowers throughout the year.

The flowers of the cocoa tree grow straight out of its trunk and branches.

Cocoa pods grow out of the trunk and branches of the cocoa tree.

Nature's gift

After a few weeks, the flowers start growing into cocoa pods. A typical tree produces about 100 cocoa pods every year. The pods are about 20 cm long and weigh about 500 grams. They range in colour from orange to purple. Each pod takes about five months to mature and holds between 40 and 60 seeds or beans. It can take between 300 and 900 beans to make a kilogram of chocolate, depending on the type of chocolate you are making.

Harvest time

The pods are picked throughout the year, but most of them are harvested between May and December. The pods are carefully cut from the tree with a machete and split open. Inside the pod are the cocoa beans, which are coated in a white substance, called pulp. The beans are spread out and covered with banana leaves. They are left for up to a week to ferment, after which they are spread out to dry in the sunshine. After two weeks, the beans are ready to be scooped into sacks and transported to factories.

The white pulp that coats cocoa beans is sticky and sweet.

The chocolate factory

Once the cocoa beans have dried and fermented, they are delivered to factories around the world. Here, they are processed in order to produce all kinds of chocolate products.

The taste of cocoa beans depends on how long they are roasted for.

Processing the beans

After the cocoa beans have been washed and sorted, they are roasted in a large revolving drum. Next, their outer shell is removed and they are heated and pressed between heavy rollers. This turns the beans into a thick, creamy liquid, called chocolate liquor. Some of the liquor is then separated into cocoa butter and a solid mass called press cake. The cocoa butter is used to make chocolate; the press cake is finely ground to make cocoa powder.

Which flavour?

In order to make chocolate, manufacturers combine chocolate liquor and cocoa butter as well as sugar, milk and, in some cases, flavourings. Dark chocolate is made without milk; the amount of milk in milk chocolate depends on how creamy it should be; white chocolate does not contain chocolate liquor, just cocoa butter, milk and sugar.

Bars of different types of chocolate contain different amounts of cocoa solid. In general, the more cocoa solid that is used, the darker the chocolate.

Conching the chocolate

When all the ingredients have been combined, the mixture is placed in a conching machine and ground down for up to 4 days to make it smooth. Next, the chocolate is put in tempering machines, which heat and cool it. This makes the chocolate shiny and silky smooth. Finally, it is ready to be moulded into sweets.

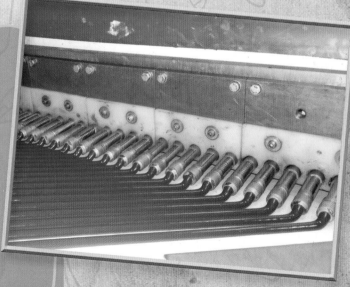

Once the chocolate has been tempered, it is melted and formed into all kinds of sweets, such as chocolate bars.

Putting chocolate on the map

Scientists believe that cocoa trees are native to the Amazon Rainforest. Ancient tribes cultivated the trees and planted them throughout Central and South America. These days, cocoa is an important cash crop and the trees are grown in many parts of the world.

Chocolate trade

Cocoa trees can only be grown in areas close to the Equator, which have a warm and wet climate throughout the year. There are cocoa plantations in South and Central America, Africa, South and Southeast Asia, and Oceania.

Chocolate production mostly takes place in Europe and North America, so the majority of cocoa beans are exported to those countries. The Republic of Côte d'Ivoire, or Ivory Coast, is the world's biggest exporter, followed by Ghana, Indonesia and Nigeria. Combined, West African countries produce 70 per cent of the world's cocoa.

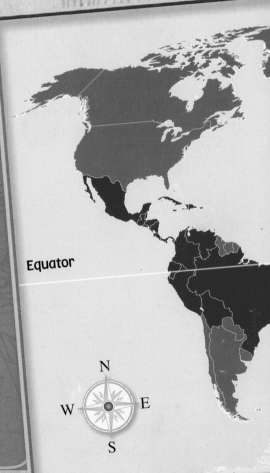

Equator

N
W   E
S

Flavour by nation

The amount of cocoa grown is not the only important factor for farmers; many compete to cultivate beans prized for their quality and flavour. The taste of cocoa beans is dependent on many factors, such as the soil, the climate and the type of bean. Every region produces cocoa with a different flavour.

When beans are left to ferment in the sunshine, it can affect the flavour of the chocolate that is produced.

Chocolate consumption

Chocolate is big business. Reports predict that the global chocolate market will grow to US$98.3 billion by 2016! Americans and Western Europeans accounted for over 70 per cent of cocoa consumed globally between 2000 and 2008. Now, chocolate consumption is increasing in countries like China and India, too.

■ Cocoa producing country

This map shows the cocoa producing countries of the world.
Currently, about 3,000,000 tonnes of cocoa is produced worldwide each year.

Fair trade chocolate

Many cocoa farmers are dependent on large chocolate companies for their income. Sometimes, the money farmers receive for their produce doesn't even cover the cost of running their farm. This can lead to poor practices, including child labour and dangerous working conditions.

This farmer is applying pesticides to a cocoa tree. The chemicals could harm his health, but many farmers cannot afford protective clothing such as goggles and masks.

Farming conditions

Over 90 per cent of cocoa farms are small, family-run businesses and often provide the only income for that family. The money these farms make from selling their produce often isn't enough to run the farm, feed the family and educate the children. This lack of income means that farming practices are often unsafe – farmers use old and dangerous tools and don't wear any protective clothing when using chemicals, such as pesticides.

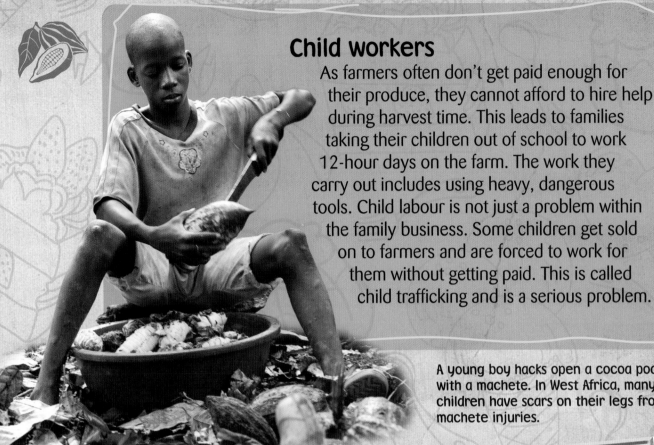

Child workers

As farmers often don't get paid enough for their produce, they cannot afford to hire help during harvest time. This leads to families taking their children out of school to work 12-hour days on the farm. The work they carry out includes using heavy, dangerous tools. Child labour is not just a problem within the family business. Some children get sold on to farmers and are forced to work for them without getting paid. This is called child trafficking and is a serious problem.

A young boy hacks open a cocoa pod with a machete. In West Africa, many children have scars on their legs from machete injuries.

Fairer for everyone

Fair trade organisations, such as the Fairtrade Foundation, help cash crop farmers to get fair payment and conditions. These organisations will ask farmers to ban child labour, provide safe working conditions, and operate in an environmentally-friendly way.

In return, the organisations ensure that farmers are paid a fair price for their produce. This means that farmers can afford health care and education for their family. Fair trade organisations also provide money for community projects such as wells for drinking water, public buildings, schools and clinics.

FAIRTRADE

The Fairtrade Foundation's symbol guarantees that farmers have been paid a fair wage for their produce.

13

Ancient food
of the gods

The first people to savour the taste of chocolate were the Mayans. This ancient civilization lived in parts of present-day Mexico and Central America from about 1800 BCE to 1500 CE.

Mayan magic beans

The ancient Mayans were enjoying chocolate as far back as the sixth century. The Mayans believed the cocoa tree was the tree of the Mayan gods and it was a gift from the gods to humans. They ate the sweet pulp surrounding the beans and made a drink called *tchacahoua* from the beans. *Tchacahoua* was drunk during religious ceremonies or given as a gift. To make *tchacahoua,* the Mayans roasted the beans in earthenware pots. Next, the beans were ground between two stones to make a powder. The powder was mixed with boiling water. Twigs, chilli, honey or ground maize were added for flavour.

The Mayans ground the cocoa beans on a small stone table called a *metate.*

'Chocolatl'

The Aztecs lived between the fourteenth and sixteenth centuries in parts of modern-day Mexico. They made a cold, spicy, frothy drink from the cocoa beans called 'chocolatl', from which the English word for chocolate stems. The Aztecs believed the god Quetzalcoatl brought the cocoa tree to Earth and showed them how to use the beans to make this nourishing drink. Chocolatl was so precious that it was reserved only for the rich and noble. Cocoa beans were also used as money. Aztec Emperors kept vaults of beans to use as currency.

An Aztec woman prepares chocolatl. Pouring the drink from a height made it frothy.

The drink of kings

Emperor Montezuma II reigned over the Aztecs from 1502 to 1520 and was known for his love of chocolate: *"The divine drink, which builds up resistance and fights fatigue. A cup of this precious drink [cocoa] permits a man to walk for a whole day without food."* He was one of the last rulers of the Aztec Empire before it was occupied by Spain. Before defeating Montezuma, the Spanish Conquistador Hernán Cortés visited him in his royal court and was served cocoa in a golden goblet. In 1527, Cortés returned to Spain with a galleon filled with cocoa beans.

An Aztec drawing of the god Quetzalcoatl bringing chocolate to humans.

Chocolate reaches Europe

Cocoa beans have a strong bitter taste and the 'chocolatl' drunk by the Aztecs would be too sharp for most people's tastes today. The Spanish added different spices and came up with their own tasty recipe.

Rich people in sixteenth-century Spain used to hold chocolate parties.

The spicy Spanish drink

After cocoa had been introduced in Spain in the sixteenth century, Spanish monks created a new chocolate drink. They roasted the beans and ground them to a powder. Then they added hot water, vanilla and spices such as cinnamon and nutmeg. Last of all, they stirred in sugar and cream.

Cocoa beans were rare and expensive so chocolate became fashionable amongst the rich. The Spanish loved their chocolate drink and managed to keep it a secret from the rest of Europe for nearly a century!

European aristocracy were served chocolate drinks from special chocolate pots.

Chocolate catches on

The Spanish couldn't keep chocolate to themselves forever. When the Spanish princesses Anne (1601–1666) and Maria Theresa (1638–1683) married into the French royal family they took their love of chocolate with them. When sugar was added to the hot drink it caught on with aristocracy throughout Europe. The first chocolate house was opened in 1657 in London, England. It was called 'The Coffee Mill and Tobacco Roll' and hot chocolate became its bestselling drink.

Powder power!

By the eighteenth century, chocolate drinks were popular in many European countries. However, roasting and grinding the beans was all still done by hand. In 1828, the Dutch inventor Casparus van Houten developed a machine to press cocoa beans. This made the cocoa powder less fatty and improved the taste of the chocolate drink. It also made adding other ingredients to the powder easier and a new recipe was developed. This was the beginning of the first eating chocolate.

The Spanish still love their chocolate. These churros taste a bit like doughnuts and are dipped into rich chocolate sauce.

Birth of the chocolate bar

In the nineteenth century, new machinery was invented that made it possible to process the first chocolate bars and chocolate sweets. Some of the chocolate companies who made the first chocolate bars are still producing chocolate today!

Weighing and Filling Packets

Women factory workers sort and pack chocolate bars at the Fry's chocolate factory in Bristol.

The first bar

British chocolate manufacturer Joseph Fry invented the first chocolate bar. The Fry family founded the chocolate company in 1761 in Bristol. At this time, chocolate was still only available as a drink. In 1847, the company founder's great grandson, Joseph Fry, discovered a way of mixing cocoa powder with melted cocoa butter and sugar to create a paste. The paste could be pressed into moulds to form chocolate bars that could be eaten.

By the nineteenth century, chocolate production in Europe became industrial. Huge steam-powered machines were used to mass-produce chocolate.

The Swiss mix

Joseph Fry's original chocolate bars tasted bittersweet. It took two Swiss manufacturers to create a tastier milk chocolate bar. For years, Daniel Peter tried adding milk to his chocolate recipe but couldn't prevent the milk in the bars from going off. In 1867, Henri Nestlé discovered a way of treating the milk so it didn't spoil. The men joined forces and in 1870, they invented the first milk chocolate bar using condensed milk. Together, they founded the world famous food company Nestlé.

Chocolate town

Two chocolate brands that launched in Victorian times were so successful that whole towns were built around them. Cadbury was founded in 1824 in Birmingham, England, by John Cadbury. In 1879, the Cadbury family built a new factory with housing for its workers in Birmingham. They named this model village Bournville. The Hershey Company was founded in 1894 in Pennsylvania, USA, by Milton Snavely Hershey. In 1906, Hershey took over the town of Derry Church in Pennsylvania. He renamed the place Hershey but it is often called Chocolatetown.

This early advertisement for Cadbury's cocoa powder recommends the drink for children, athletes and the elderly.

19

Is chocolate good for you?

Chocolate contains sugar and fat, so it should be eaten as a treat. But small amounts of dark chocolate can also be good for you. So what is healthy and what is unhealthy about chocolate?

Healthy

- Chocolate can make us feel better. Experts have found that eating small amounts of dark chocolate produces chemicals in our brains that block pain and reduce stress.

- Researchers have found that chemicals found in dark chocolate could help to protect the body from heart disease.

- Scientists have discovered that one of the ingredients in dark chocolate can help stop a persistent cough.

- In tests, Italian scientists found that eating 100g of dark chocolate each day can lower blood pressure and can help to control diabetes.

Unhealthy

- Chocolate is high in fat (cocoa butter), sugar and carbohydrate. Eating too much chocolate without doing any exercise might make you put on weight.

- Chocolate does not contain many nutrients.

- Chocolate is bad for your teeth. The sugar in chocolate forms plaque which causes tooth decay.

- Chocolate can cause headaches. Ingredients in chocolate have been found to trigger headaches in migraine sufferers.

Dark chocolate only has health benefits when it is eaten in small amounts.

Chocolate celebrations

Chocolate is often given as a gift on birthdays, Christmas, Easter, Valentine's Day and special days like Mother's Day and Father's Day. Many countries around the world even host chocolate festivals!

Easter eggs

One of the most popular times for giving and receiving chocolate is Easter. Chocolate eggs first caught on in the nineteenth century when chocolatiers learned how to mould eating chocolate. The idea probably originated in Germany and France. Cadbury didn't produce its first chocolate eggs until 1875. Once they started producing milk chocolate eggs, the tradition really caught on in Britain. These days, Easter eggs come in all sizes and people enjoy chocolate bunnies and chicks, too.

Fabulous festivals

There are lots of fun festivals that celebrate our love of chocolate. Britain and the USA celebrate National Chocolate Week each year. In Britain, it kicks off every October. There are exhibitions, chocolate-making events, competitions and tastings all over the country. Similar celebrations take place throughout the USA in March.

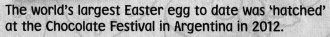
The world's largest Easter egg to date was 'hatched' at the Chocolate Festival in Argentina in 2012.

Chocolate art

The Festival Internacional de Chocolate in Portugal is a chocolate lover's dream. It takes place every Easter in the medieval town of Óbidos. Kids enjoy the Children's House of Chocolate where they can make all kinds of chocolate recipes. There are competitions to find the 'Chocolate of the Year' and 'Best International Chocolate Recipe.' The highlight of the festival is the exhibition of chocolate sculptures.

One of the amazing chocolate sculptures on display at the chocolate festival in Óbidos, Portugal.

Chocolate-dipped strawberries

Strawberries dipped in chocolate make a great Mother's Day or Father's Day gift. Plus, they are quick and easy to make.

You will need:

Ingredients

Fresh strawberries

Milk, plain or white eating chocolate

Cake decorations such as sprinkles

Equipment

Small saucepan

Small heat-proof bowl that fits inside the saucepan

Baking tray

Grease-proof paper

Large metal spoon

1 Wash the strawberries, pat them dry and arrange on a baking tray covered with grease-proof paper.

2 Heat about six cm of water in the saucepan until it simmers. Turn the heat to low.

3 Break up the chocolate into squares and put them in the bowl.

Place the bowl of chocolate over the saucepan of simmering water.

Stir the chocolate until it has melted. Turn off the heat.

4 Using oven gloves, carefully remove the bowl from the saucepan. Hold each strawberry by the stem and dip into the melted chocolate. Next, dip the strawberries in sprinkles or other decorations.

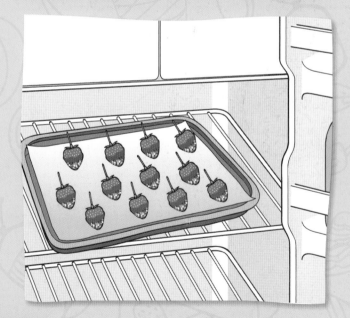

5 Place the strawberries back on the baking tray. Pop the baking tray in the refrigerator until the chocolate has set.

Yummy careers

How can you make a living from working with chocolate? One way is to become a chocolatier – a person who makes confectionery from chocolate.

Chocolatiers create many new kinds of chocolates.

The life of a chocolatier

Holly Caulfield is an artist and loves chocolate. At her shop Chocoholly in Hove, East Sussex, England, she is able to combine her passion for chocolate with her artistic skills.

Q What made you decide to become a chocolatier?

A I saw the film 'Chocolat'. I realised that chocolate was a mystery to me. I set off on a quest to discover more. I began by making my own chocolates. I liked adding new flavours and creating beautiful looking chocolates.

Q How did you start your business?

A I started off at home, working in my kitchen. I was soon supplying my handmade chocolates to some major stores. So in 2011, I opened the shop.

Q What's your favourite part of the job?

A Eating and tasting the chocolate! I love hand-painting and thinking up new ways of presenting the chocolates, too. Easter time is really exciting for me, it's also my busiest time of year. This year, I'm making giant hand-painted eggs – they weigh about 10 kg and are 90 cm tall!

Q What's the hardest part of your job?

A Book-keeping! And, sometimes the hours are long.

Q What are your tips to wannabe chocolatiers?

A Love your food. Get into cooking and eating different foods from an early age. Always strive to eat the best quality food you can find.

Visit the Chocoholly website to see the chocolatey works of art that Holly creates: www.chocoholly.com

Facts and figures

H ave you had your fill of chocolate yet? No, then here are some fun facts, trivia, and some bite-sized bits about chocolate to satisfy you all...

M&Ms for soldiers

The American chocolate manufacturer Mars created M&Ms in 1940 for soldiers going to fight in World War II. The candy-coated chocolates were popular because they didn't melt in people's hands.

Cocoa power

The French leader Napoleon Bonaparte ate chocolate to give him his energy whenever he went to war.

The average person eats 10,000 chocolate bars in their lifetime!

Sixty-six per cent of chocolate is consumed between meals.

Chocolate record

The world's biggest-ever chocolate bar was made by English chocolate makers Thorntons in 2011. The company made the whopping four-metre long bar to commemorate one hundred years of production. The giant bar weighed nearly six tonnes!

Chocolate millions

The top three manufacturers of chocolate in the world are Kraft Foods (USA), Mars Inc (USA) and Nestlé S.A. (Switzerland). Kraft, which includes the Cadbury brand, made net sales of US$19,965 million in 2011.

Chocolate vs fruit

There is more protein in a bar of dark chocolate than in a banana. And dark chocolate contains more antioxidants than strawberries!

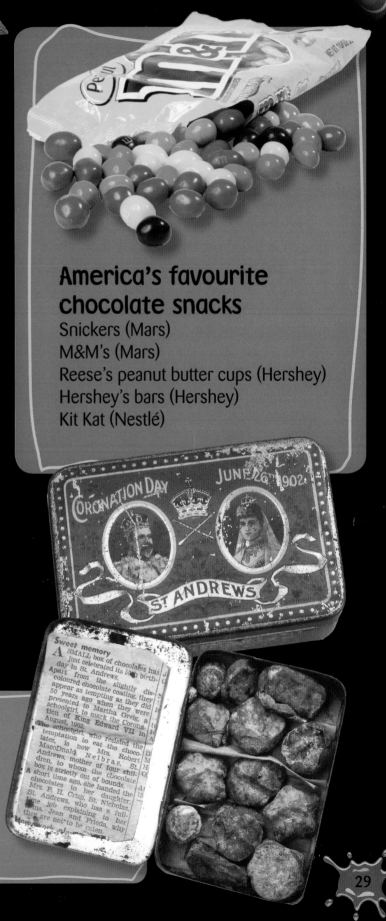

America's favourite chocolate snacks

Snickers (Mars)
M&M's (Mars)
Reese's peanut butter cups (Hershey)
Hershey's bars (Hershey)
Kit Kat (Nestlé)

Some of the bestselling chocolate sweets from around the world:

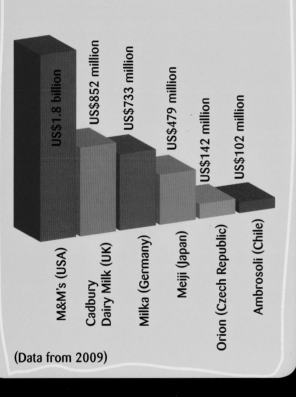

- US$1.8 billion — M&M's (USA)
- US$852 million — Cadbury Dairy Milk (UK)
- US$733 million — Milka (Germany)
- US$479 million — Meiji (Japan)
- US$142 million — Orion (Czech Republic)
- US$102 million — Ambrosoli (Chile)

(Data from 2009)

Ancient sweets

Is this the oldest box of chocolates? These chocolates were made to commemorate the coronation of King Edward VII in 1902. They were discovered in St Andrews, Scotland.

Glossary

Antioxidants Substances, such as vitamin C, that help the body's defence system.

Aristocracy The upper classes of society.

Blood pressure The pressure of blood against the walls of blood vessels as it circulates around the body.

Canopy The top layer in a forest, formed by the crowns or tops of trees.

Cash crop A crop, such as cocoa or tobacco, which is grown to be sold rather than consumed by the farmer or its livestock.

Chocolatier A person who makes or sells chocolate.

Civilization A society or culture at a particular time in history.

Cocoa butter The yellow, fatty solid extracted from cocoa beans that is used to make chocolate, soap and cosmetics.

Condensed milk Canned milk that has been thickened and sweetened.

Cultivate To look after and care for a plant.

Diabetes A medical condition affecting some people that means there is too much sugar in their blood and urine. It can be treated by changing diet or taking a hormone called insulin.

Evergreen Having green leaves all year.

Export To transport goods to another country in order for them to be sold.

Ferment To carry out a process in which a substance breaks down or changes into something else. Cocoa beans are fermented to develop the chocolate flavour.

Galleon A Spanish warship used from the fifteenth to the seventeenth century.

Harvest The time or season when crops are gathered.

Indigenous Describes a tree or plant that grows naturally in a particular area or environment.

Machete A heavy, curved knife that is used for cutting crops.

Medieval Belonging to or to do with the Middle Ages.

Migraine A severe headache.

Native Originally grown or born in a particular place.

Oceania The area that includes the islands of the Pacific Ocean and the surrounding seas.

Pesticides Substance for killing harmful insects and other pests.

Plantations Large areas of land where crops such as coffee, tea or chocolate are grown.

Plaque The sticky film on teeth that is formed by sugar and contains bacteria that harms teeth and gums.

Revolving Turning in a circle around a central point.

Tropical To do with the area that is close to the Equator.

Further reading

Fiction

Charlie and the Chocolate Factory by Roald Dahl, Puffin (2007)

The Whizz Pop Chocolate Shop by Kate Saunders, Marion Lloyd Books (2012)

The Chocolate Touch by Patrick Skene Catling, HarperTrophy (2006)

The Chocolate Tree: A Mayan Folktale by Linda Lowery and Richard Keep, Millbrook Press (2009)

Chocolate Box Girls (various titles) by Cathy Cassidy, Puffin (2012)

Non-fiction

A Chocolate Bar: How It's Made by Sarah Ridley, Franklin Watts (2009)

How is Chocolate Made? by Angela Royston, Heinemann Library (2005)

The Story of Chocolate by Caryn Jenner, Dorling Kindersley (2005)

Totally Triffic Chocolate by Clive Goddard, Scholastic (2010)

Recipe books

Professor Cook's Mind-blowing Bakes by Lorna Brash, Wayland (2012)

Covered in Chocolate by Lizzie Lou, Tate Publishing & Enterprises (2009)

My Chocolate Year: A Novel with 12 Recipes by Charlotte Herman, Simon & Schuster Children's Publishing (2008)

Roald Dahl's Revolting Recipes by Roald Dahl, Red Fox Picture Books (1996)

Websites

Cadbury: www.cadbury.co.uk

Hershey's: www.hersheys.com

The Fairtrade Foundation: www.fairtrade.org.uk

International Cocoa Organization: www.icco.org

World Cocoa Foundation: www.worldcocoafoundation.org/who-we-are

Index